Grandma's Little Book of Inspirational Poems

Leatha Augustus

Dedicated to all my grandkids with love!

Shankayla, Ja'Tara, Jasmin, Chante, Tierra, Renee, Tejana, Ethan, Darius, Ravyn, Shiann, Delana, Damon J., TJ, David

Table of Contents

Time

Time doesn't stand still

And we can't go back in time.

We must move, endure, and conquer

Things of the past.

For soon there will be no more.

God has given us power over our own spirits.

We must use that power well

Because in the past, we cannot dwell.

We can't grow or become strong

Because our enemy, the devil, won't leave us alone.

We must work while it is day.

The night is upon us.

In whom will we trust?

Our time will soon end.

What then? What then?

God knows and sees all.

All we need to do is heed His call.

Things happen we don't know why

But we can't let time pass us by.

Time will not and cannot wait.

So, lets hurry, for goodness' sake:

Time is about to end

What then? What then?

God help us all.

The End……

God Will

It's not where you begin to change,

It's where the change takes you.

We travel life's road of uncertainty.

We know not where we head

But we will not stumble, if by God we're led.

He said, "I am the way, follow me.

Where you are blinded, I can see,

I haven't given you the spirit of fear,

Call out to me, I'm right here.

If you'll believe, I'll make things right

And when you are free, hold on tight

Because the enemy works day and night."

Your words sound good to man

But on God's word you have to stand.

When you feel weak and all alone,

God said, "Let the weak be strong."

Someone is always praying for you.

Follow Your Goals

Life isn't always what you want it to be

Or even what it seems to be

But follow your goals.

You don't have to be old

To experience life's stumbling blocks and holes.

Just follow your goals.

It's not all about fame and wealth or idolizing
someone else.

Your life is all about yourself.

Follow your goals.

When things crumble all around you, don't lose sight,

Grab on to life and hold tight

And follow your goals.

There is nothing you can't do.

Listen to your parents, but it's all up to you.

Nothing in this world is free,

Even though it seems to be.

Don't ever let us hear you say,

This price it too hard to pay.

So, follow your goals.

What More

What more are you asking of me?

I am so tired, can't you see?

I do my very best for you

But you can't see what I do.

Take your eyes off yourself

And try to see someone else.

Sometimes, I feel like a big oak tree

That the wear of time has decreased

But I'm getting stronger day by day,

As long as I let Him lead the way.

So, follow my lead as I follow Him

And others will say I'll follow them.

My tiredness will soon be gone

'Cause I'll follow Him all the way home.

It's Harvest Time

We sit, we weep, our tears fall to the floor.

We begin to wonder can we take much more.

Our body aches, but our spirit aches more.

The children of old was put in the mire

But in this day, we have to go through the fire.

Souls are dying in the harvest field,

The hungry are dying without a meal.

We are lights and we have to shine

Because Jesus said, "All souls are mine."

Do we think by serving God, we're all set?

We haven't endured to the end yet.

There are fires we still must go through,

So that the lost can come to you.

Help us to reach, reach, reach

Around every corner, and down every street.

Our hands stretched out to reach someone.

Some mother's daughter, some daddy's son.

The ant is wise, and we must be too.

So, we trust God to lead us to you.

If we would only abide in His will,

When storms arise, He'll say peace be still.

In the word of God, we've been told:

Feed my sheep and win my souls.

Your ears haven't heard, your eyes can't behold

Your reward will not be in silver or gold

But life eternal.

Amen.

Just Believe

Where there's turmoil,

Believe in serenity.

Where there's infirmity,

Believe in health.

Where there's heartache,

Believe in love.

Where there's confusion,

Believe in knowledge.

Where there's weakness,

Believe in strength,

Where there's betrayal,

Believe in loyalty.

Where there's war,

Believe in peace.

Where there's separation,

Believe in togetherness.

Where there's one,

Believe in you.

Believe that you can…

<u>You and Me</u>

I cared for you when you didn't.

I kept pushing you when you thought of quitting.

I helped you when you wouldn't.

I encouraged you when you couldn't.

When I felt your pain, I prayed.

I could have turned my back but I stayed.

Behind every dark cloud, there's a brighter day.

Follow directions, you'll find the way.

The door to a successful life is open wide.

All you have to do is step inside.

You think you are living but you're only existing.

It's the realness of life that you are missing.

Step into the light and give it a try.

Your life is not what it could be and I know why.

That's why you should reach for the sky.

It's not where or when you start,

As long as you do it from the heart.

Life isn't measured in money amounts,

It's where you end up that counts.

Do what you know to do and do it well

And the benefits you reap, they will tell.

Change your life for only you.

Then others will know they can do it too.

I'm always here for you.

The Miracle Inside

When you see God's child with his head hung low,

Not even knowing where to go,

Take him by his hand and pull him aside.

Tell him about Jesus, the miracle inside.

The world is searching for something,

Not knowing what they find- the wrong thing.

They are looking for a place to hide

And here we stand with the miracle inside.

The terrorists have given our nation a scare.

They're praying now but soon they won't care.

The turmoil and wars will never cease

But I know a place where there's always peace.

One of the seven sins is the sin of lust.

But we say "Our nation stands on: In God we trust."

Our sons and daughters fight side by side.

Did we tell them about Jesus, the miracle inside?

We don't have to fear nor doubt.

Jesus knew this would happen so, there's a way out

For you, Jesus died.

Now in you, He's the miracle inside.

Accept your miracle.

In God's Hands Now

In my heart, no one can take your place

Because I love you in a very special way.

In my hands, God entrusted you to me

And let me know, what would be, will be and

I've not always liked the things you've done

But I'll always love you, my daughters and sons.

It's not how the world sees you

Or even how you see yourself.

I'm going to hold on to you

'Til there's nothing left.

I've dangled you on my knees

Now, I carry you in my heart.

Whether here or there, we will never be apart.

You've gone your own ways,

Whether right or wrong.

My desire for you is that you come back home.

Not to my house but the house of God,

Where you were raised on the word of the Lord.

Into the future, God could see.

That's why He chose to give you to me.

No matter what happens, come what may,

This is one thing you can always say:

Mama loves me.

God & Man

What has God done to thee, O Man

That thou would turn your back?

Do you not know, that the promises of God are not slack?

He died on the cross for you.

He said, "I overcome

And you can too.

Stop, my son and turn around.

I'm coming soon

And I don't want to leave you behind.

What, my son, have I done?

For your sins I gave, my son,

Please don't crucify me afresh.

For I love you, that's why I brought those tests

Man will hurt you, and cause you to fail

But look and see the nails

In my hands and in my feet.

They're for you my son, not to suffer defeat.

So, come on, son and don't give up.

Even I had to drink the bitter cup.

If you'll hold on, you will see.

I will come and abide with thee

And all the things you've gone through,

Will not compare to what I'll do for you.

You're not my servant but you're my friend.

So run this race until you win!

I'm coming soon!

God Has A Plan

God has a plan.

He's trying to teach man

To abide by His will

And realize that He is God still,

No matter what it looks like.

God's plan is right on track.

Repent, America, repent.

Pray for our next president,

Just like in the days of old.

Disobedience is sin, God will react.

It's not just a bible story, it's a fact.

The war pots are beginning to boil.

America, we're in great turmoil.

Who will be the next president?

It's not in the hands of man.

Vote and do your part

Then leave it in the hands of God.

Can't you see that God has a plan?

Whether Romney or Obama,

God will choose the man.

It's Time

We are living in the time of the end.

It's time to repent for our sins.

Jesus is coming but we don't know when.

The signs of the times we can see.

The will of God is where we should be.

To be hid under the shadow of His wings,

To be kept from ungodly things,

To walk in His light

That shines so bright

And to love Him with all our might.

He will take all your trouble away

Then you will be able to say,

"To know Him is to love Him.

He is the Pearl of Great Price.

He is such a precious gem.

The whole world needs to serve Him."

So, make up your mind.

This is the time,

'Cause we are living in the

Time of the end.

God's Will

I will calm your storm.

I will deliver you.

I will save your household.

I will destroy the work of the enemy.

I will never leave you.

I will go with you, even to the end of the world.

I will turn it around.

I will carry your burden.

I will give peace in the midst of confusion.

I will not remember your past, if you repent.

I will stick closer than a brother.

I will solve your problems.

I will bless you.

I will raise up a standard.

I will make a way of escape.

I will defeat the enemy.

I will supply your need.

I will give you the desires of your heart.

I will and I am.

The Test

These last few years have been hard

But you have made it by the power of God.

He brought you out of darkness into the light.

Hold on to Him with all of your might

'Cause you are a precious flower in His sight.

There are times you've felt He did not care

But the Lord has always been there.

His arms around you, you can feel,

His love for you is oh so real.

Keep your faith in Him always

Because these are the last days.

His love for you is purer than snow.

He died for you, and this we know

That His love is stronger than death.

We're all being tried, so pass the test.

The time of testing is about to end.

God's people are sure to win.

So, look up now and rejoice.

Listen to the wind, you'll hear His voice.

This test of life is almost done.

By My strength, you'll overcome.

So, praise Me now and be at peace

And never let your love for Me cease.

Who Am I?

You don't know who I am.

You don't know what I'm about.

The things I feel in my heart

Or the way I will live my life.

You think I will pattern my life after other young people.

Why not give me a chance?

Let me prove to you who I am.

I am your son, your daughter.

Teach me and I will learn.

Love me and I will love.

You gave me life.

Don't tell me what to do, show me how.

Trust that I will change.

Don't let what I say or do confuse you.

It's really my cry for help.

Don't judge me, just love me with unconditional love.

My heart aches, my mind is confused

But this too will pass.

It's like a cloudy day with no sunshine in view.

I sleep, I awake, tomorrow will be new.

I can see it, I can feel it, but mostly I just know it.

Watch me crawl, watch me walk, watch me begin a new life.

Thanks for caring.

-Your child.

Where Is Heaven?

Heaven is not so far away.

It's not always in the sky.

If we have love from day to day,

Heaven is in our life.

The earth is the Lord's

And everything there in.

We must live right so, there is no room for sin.

Look to the hills, your help will surely come

And shade you from the wind and rain.

It will keep you in the storm.

Children, the end is upon us.

The time is drawing nigh

But if you're in Christ, you will go to sleep.

You will not die.

Heaven on earth is the place to be.

Such love, such joy, such peace.

For heaven is not so far away.

It's right here on earth with me.

Not Winning

With what's happening right now,

The devil thinks he's winning.

He's standing back now and grinning.

He has the people of this world fooled

But the Christians know that God rules.

The devil can't do anything God won't allow

But that won't stop him from continuing to try.

He thought he had won with Adam and Eve

So, he has come again to try and deceive.

Open your eyes, world and see what's going on.

Rejoice now and sing a new song.

One of happiness, peace, and love

That can only come from above.

This is not the end yet.

God didn't say so.

When that time comes, the whole world will know.

This pandemic has been very hard

But it doesn't have power over God.

We have to trust Him, do what's right

'Cause he's coming soon,

Morning, noon or night.

As for me, I'm going to be alright.

Persevere

Who am I? I'm trying to find myself.

I'm tired of trying to be someone else.

I wake up and wonder, is this the day?

I do know I wasn't born this way,

Things happen I don't understand.

Am I on my own or am I in God's hand?

I know my life is not my own,

From God, it is just a loan

But He paid a price I could never pay.

When He bled and died on the cross that day,

I know He loves me; His word says so.

This is something everyone should know.

Who am I? I'm a child of the King.

A King above all other kings.

So why do I feel all alone?

Is it because what I'm doing is wrong?

I will do better, 'cause I know I can.

All I have to do is take hold of His hand,

It's getting clear to me now,

I am a strong young person.

I am going in the right direction now.

Others look at me and say tell me how,

I didn't think you could take it,

I didn't think you would make it,

But look at you now.

You are becoming who you should be.

Now everyone around you can see.

I know who you are.

You are strong.

You're trying to stop doing wrong.

Give yourself the benefit of doubt.

You are who God made you to be.

Love

Love is not just a four-letter word.

It's not something you've heard.

It's caring unconditionally

That goes beyond our thoughts.

Love comes from God

So, let love abide

With your heart opened wide.

When your life is being tested

It's because love has been manifested.

Tests of life come to make us stronger.

The test won't be any longer

'Cause peace and joy comes with love.

I seen love come in many ways.

When trouble comes, love stays.

If love could talk,

You would hear it say:

I'm yours forever

You can feel love and sometimes

You can see it.

Love is gentle and kind

But most of all, love is mine.

The Darkness

Sometimes, you'll feel like your day is dark…

The darkness seems to overtake you.

You say within yourself: What should I do?

What you do is look for the light.

Though darkness surrounds you, the light shines through.

Do not despair or be afraid

Because that's not how we were made.

So, don't let darkness take the win.

The light of life is your friend.

If you walk with your friend,

You will always see your way.

Not only during hard times

But all through the day.

Hang on to the stars and hold on tight.

Look to Jesus, He'll make everything right.

You think to yourself nothing is the same

But my God said, He'll never change.

I've heard people say the struggle is real.

It's not the struggle, it's how you feel.

You're not invincible because of your age.

Every day you wake up, you turn a new page.

It's time now for every girl and every boy to lift their hands and leap for joy.

It's a cold dark world we live in.

You know why? It's because of sin.

Sin brings darkness and darkness blinds.

The light is coming and the light shines.

Look up and live.

www.ingramcontent.com/pod-product-compliance
Lightning Source LLC
Chambersburg PA
CBHW020441030426
42337CB00014B/1343